Mudslide
WHEN IT ALL FALLS DOWN

By

MARY MASON FOOTE

Copyright © 2018; 2019; 2020 Mary Mason Foote

All rights reserved. No part of this publication may be reproduced, distributed, or transmitted in any form or by any means, including photocopying, recording, or other electronic or mechanical methods, without the prior written permission of the publisher, except in the case of brief quotations embodied in critical reviews and certain other noncommercial uses permitted by copyright law.

ISBN: 978-1-951300-82-1

Liberation's Publishing LLC
West Point, Mississippi
www.liberationspublishing.com

Mudslide

WHEN IT ALL FALLS DOWN

By

MARY MASON FOOTE

Dedication

I dedicate this book to Life (Living in Faith Every day) you have allowed me to grow into survival mode. You have taught me how to give and receive at the same time, without losing my mind. You coach me every day, as the woman who has grown tremendously in your path, a few knockdowns and blows that brought me to my knees in agony, but hey that comes with every breath taker that lives.

Mary Mason Foote

Acknowledgments

I would like to thank ALMIGHTY GOD, if it wasn't for Him, there is no way I could have made it through the many difficult times. Jesus's life literally saved mines. It was God who collected and is still collecting my tears. As I sit and think about things for a moment, I close my eyes just to say thanks for Heaven's rain. I thank God, for my husband Vincent, being married to him was a blessing and training grounds that prepared me for God's purpose.

I thank my number #1's My Mother Edna Ruth Mason and Two Sisters, Tonya Lewis and Thelma Shaw those three keep me straight. My two seeds of love and the coolest children, my son Malik Sanders and daughter Tyler Sanders. My Father Ezell Mason. My big brother, Anthony Ezell (BIG HACK) Brown. May he Rest in Peace (9/19/2019) thanks for always protecting.

To my friends and those who encouraged me in the darkest of times, I thank you for your comfort and support, whether good, bad, or fake love, it all helped me to be strong.

Mary Mason Foote

Contents

Introduction 11

Here He Comes 13

Give It A Try 17

Full Blown Courtship 23

The Move 27

The Green-Eyed Devil 31

Holidays 33

Getting to Know Him 35

Going Deeper 39

I Have to Get Out of This 41

Lunch 45

Happily, Ever after 49

Emotional Rollercoaster 53

Trying to Escape 55

Moving 59

Narcissist 65

You Never Know When It's Your Last Time 67

When It All Falls Down 71

The Last Breath 77

Phone Calls and Funeral Plans 83

Plague Thoughts 91

About the Author 93

Epilogue 95

Introduction

In 2009, I wrote a four-page letter to God, describing the type of man that I would love to marry. In 2008 divorce from the first husband of ten years and if you count our courtship fifteen years of my life. It was either I kill him or divorce him, honey, I chose to divorce him. Currently, I have no regrets about that decision. That chapter of my life taught me how to forgive and let a person have what they want. The heart wants what the heart wants. I want to encourage every one of you. If you're dealing with unforgiveness, please forgive people! Our Almighty God in Heaven forgave us, even before we knew we needed Him. FORGIVE, LET IT GO, and LIVE YOUR ONE LIFE SWEETHEART.

Now back to this four-page letter to God. My second husband fits my letter bulletin by bulletin all except for one thing. That one thing was he wasn't buffed, and he wasn't a big guy, but he did have a little muscle tone going on. Although that wasn't a deal-breaker. I wrote it down for just fun. All of that being said, he was it, bulletin by bulletin. In hindsight what I should have written down was temper. That he had in a supersized way. He would go from zero to one hundred in a second. Making his point noticeably clear, he was right and that was it. Lord, I had so many fun and crazy times with that man that sometimes I just snicker and laugh to myself.

While reading this book, I hope that you laugh with me, cry with me, and be healed with me.

Enjoy!

Here He Comes

I wrote my letter to God and placed it in my bible. Sometime later, it appeared that my written request was coming to pass. I would often talk to God in my mind and I would tell Him, how I wanted my husband to be revealed to me. I remember saying, "Lord, I want my future husband to come into my salon, put his number in my pocket and walk back out."

October 2011 that's exactly what happened.

Vincent came into the salon, said hello to everyone, reached into my pocket and walked back out. He didn't say one word to me, no eye contact and not even a formal hey. Though my curiosity was raging, I didn't check to see what he had put in my pocket until after I had finished working. I held out until after work and when I looked, it was his phone number.

I waited to call him as long as I could. Two days later I gave in. He was so handsome and very respectable. When I did call him, he was waiting to get a haircut and asked if I could come where he was. I knew the place, so I said "yes" and went over. Even with the hair all over his face and in great need of a haircut, he still looked good. So, we sat in the car just chit-chatting until it was time for him to sit in the barber's chair. I smiled nonchalantly while deep inside hiding my excitement of possibly a new relationship forming. I was cool and handled it cute, like a pro. When I left to go back to work, I just knew that we'd be talking again soon.

As predicted, he called, and I liked it. I really can't remember what we talked about, but he did ask me if he could come over, and I said "yes." He arrived a little while later, wearing a brown suede outfit, nice boots, and a beer in his hand (really). Fly as can be and would continue to be sharp throughout our entire courtship. I loved looking at that man.

Standing there smiling at me looking as cute as ever. It was nice to have someone to talk to, and I guess that was our first date. We sat on the couch eating steamed shrimp, him sipping on his beer and watching tv. Later that night, he fell asleep in my lap. I left him lying there and went into my bedroom, not alarmed at all because I trusted him.

What I didn't explain before was that Vincent and I go way back to 1988 when we moved to Mississippi from Chicago. We dated when I was fifteen, he was my first boyfriend here in MS, and the first guy to buy me gifts. Christmas, my birthday which is in January and for Valentine's Day yes, at fifteen years of age, he was a gentleman and buying gifts. While dating me, he made sure I got a gift for every occasion. What's so funny to me is, I don't remember when or why we stopped dating and talking to one another. I didn't see him any more during our high school years, and the school wasn't that big.

I trusted him, so I went to my bedroom to get ready for bed, I put on my pajamas, and went to sleep. Later on, I heard him in my bathroom and when he came out, he had the nerves to ease on the other side of my bed without asking for permission. He spooned up behind me in an oh so gentle way. Our chemistry was undeniable; I was breathing hard but scared at the same time. He kissed me, and it was over. That brown suede suit became a floored brown suede suit, honey, yes!

Morning came. Vincent went into the bathroom and dropped a load. "Oh no he didn't just poop in my bathroom!" From that moment, I was completely turned off and to top it all off, he had the nerves to get back in the bed with me. In my mind, I was like, "boy if you don't get out of my bed, and you better not touch me either!"

We talked for a few more minutes, then he left to get ready for church. Vincent invited me to go with him and I did. I couldn't really hear or pay attention to the preacher for looking at him. I was thinking, "How are you ushering, and we just finished sinning?" Nevertheless, he worked his post and I worked my eyes just staring at him throughout service. After church, he kissed me and that was it. I loved him and left him alone after that, he became my one nightstand. Really Mary?

From November until June I would talk to him off and on but never sleep with him again. We would talk on the phone, and he would often come by the house, but I continued to give him the cold shoulder.

Mary Mason Foote

Give It A Try

It was Valentine's Day 2012 and here comes Vincent with a basket full of valentine's goodies. He was so thoughtful, but I still wouldn't budge on dating him. There was a stuffed teddy bear (dog) inside and another nice goody. I took the bear out, hugged it and placed it on my bed. From 2/14/2012, that night and every night, I would sleep with my teddy dog in my arms. If I went out of town, my doggy was going with me. Sometimes, Vincent would take my dog and put it under his arm, and I would snatch it back, saying, "nope, that's mine." It's beside me right now while I'm writing this book.

My family was already very fond of Vincent and so was I, despite the fact I wouldn't date him. In April of 2012, I had surgery and My mom stayed with me until I was able to move around good. She loves me and I love her (my mother is amazing). Here he comes, of course, my mom lets him come into the bedroom where I was. Anyone that's had surgery knows, the last thing you want is someone standing over you, especially a man, you're not dating.

He came to see me faithfully, then one day Vincent took me by the hand, looked in my eyes while he was standing over me saying, "let me take care of you. You can tell your mom to go home, and I'll take care of you." The way he looked at me and the way he said it just melted my heart. I still didn't budge though. He sat down, still holding my hand, and just looking into my eyes. He was so serious. I just knew I was special to him and he really wanted to take care of me. I smiled and was very flattered, but I still refused to date him.

A few months passed and he consistently pursued me. In his mind, I do believe he thought we were already in a relationship. I had accepted my calling from God, and on June 3rd I had my embarkation (first sermon). Vincent came and sat on the front row like we were really dating. I didn't acknowledge him being there, and to this day, I wish I hadn't overlooked him. At the time I thought "if I overlook him, he will leave me alone", but NOPE IT DIDN'T WORK! He waited, so on June 26, 2012, I finally said yes to dating him. We were like teenagers all over again. With his big pretty eyes, thick eyelashes, and beautiful smile; he always made my heart leap.

One day, we were sitting in his cousin's yard talking and his phone rang. I looked at him and he looked at me as if he was asking me if he should answer it or not. He finally did, and I heard a woman's voice.

"What are you doing," she asked.

"Sitting here with my sweetie," he replied looking straight ahead.

I laughed as he replied once again, "Sitting here with my sweetie."

I knew the woman was caught off guard and gave him a head snap as she replied back "What!!!" I chuckled as he ended the call. I assured him that it was okay. We weren't a couple until a few weeks ago and those seven months he was trying to get a yes from me didn't count. He was fair game to any woman, but now, he's mine. We laughed and he was relieved that I didn't get mad at him. One thing was for certain, Vincent respected me, and he could see that I wasn't a nagging woman, smart mouth yes, but not nagging.

See, I should've been nervous and jealous, because I almost lost him to another woman. I was the one he chose, so again If anyone should have been jealous, it should've been me and not him. I was soon to find out that there was something I should've been concerned about, but not for reasons you would think.

Okay, I was in my salon at the shampoo bowl shampooing a client's hair and talking on the phone to Vince, and I heard the Lord whisper in a soft yet alarming voice, "Abraham and Sarah." I looked puzzled, looked at the phone and said " Vincent, are you still married" and he said, "No." I knew that he had been married, but I hadn't talked to him in over ten years. I would see him sometimes in passing and since his daughter was my niece's cousin, there were times I would see him at my niece's birthday parties and I would speak, but never a lengthy conversation.

Seeing that he approached me, I figured he couldn't still be married. Honey, he was, and it was three months later when I found out.

See, I have a friend that is like Nancy Drew and she keeps me in the loop about everything in the streets. We're on the phone for what seems like twenty-four-seven. The two of us were just talking away, then she tells me to be careful because people were watching both of us. I thought, "watching us for what?" She went on to tell me she heard that he wasn't divorced.

"Quit playing!"

"I'm for real," she laughed.

I felt so cheap, betrayed, dirty and literally blown away! Here I am, with someone else's husband, I was so hurt. A lot of things started to make sense. The looks and all of the small-town talk dancing around in the people's ears. I asked Vincent again, telling him what I heard, but I didn't tell him where I got my information from. He just said "no", and their divorce was final. I believed him and I said "okay," laid in his arms and watched TV.

I mentioned it to my friend again and she told me that I could find out at the courthouse because the records are public. Oh, I couldn't wait to see. I went to the courthouse to check the public records. I searched mines first, looked at it and I was definitely divorced. I did it for the heck of it. I searched Vincent's and oh boy, what a slap in the face again! My findings, he filed but it was pending. Seeing that he put forth the effort to get the ball rolling. I wasn't 100% mad. I was 99% disappointed. I felt like he should've let it be my decision if I wanted to date him knowing that he was still married but separated pending divorce.

A lot of things started to make sense, I now understood why he would never drive his truck over to my house. He would walk and I didn't think much of it because he was living with his cousin not too far from where I lived.

Vincent would always walk to my house as if he was strolling by. After I confronted him again about my suspicious findings at the courthouse, he just looked, then he said to me "I just talked to my lawyer and he said that it was final," but he could contact him again.

I looked at him and laughed, by that time, my heart was in full effect for him, so I just patiently waited for his divorce to be final. I loved everything about him, so forgiving him was easy and yes, he apologized, but you know how that goes. He kissed and hugged me as if he was so sorry and I let him have it, but I didn't let him go.

Mary Mason Foote

Full Blown Courtship

Dating Vincent was really a task and getting to know him was strange, but I loved it! My husband's mannerisms were A1! He would open up the doors for me and boy could he clean a house. Vincent had no issues with relaxing and chilling with my family at our family gatherings, his interactions with them were cool, especially with my brother. He loved my children; he would make sure my car was clean and I had gas. He was a provider, always wining and dining me, complimenting me which kept a smile on my face. He would rub my feet and we would spend countless hours talking about the Bible (wow, I'm smiling from ear to ear). He showed me so much love and affection!

When Vincent met my children, they were teenagers 14 and 16, They respected him, but didn't understand him. Of course, they gave him the utmost respect, and I thank God for that. There was never a time when I felt uneasy about Vincent being around my children, especially my daughter which was a great concern for me. I thank the Lord for that.

Dating him was going pretty well until I saw "Old jealousy". Oh my, that is an ugly spirit. The first time I met that side of my husband was quite interesting. My son called and said that his car was running hot, so Vincent and I drove to the store where he was parked. When I got there, my ex-husband was there working on the car. My daughter got out of the car and walked over to where everyone was standing. I didn't get out, because I felt it was disrespectful, even though we were only dating, respect goes a long way in a relationship.

I sat in the car trying to talk to Mr. Foote (Vincent) that's what I called him when I could see that he was irritated. He's sitting there with his fingertips pressed against his beautiful full lips, eyes red and a little pouting. He sat there quietly, looking straight ahead and I asked, "baby are you okay?" He didn't budge a bit, nor did he say one word! So, I just looked and said to myself, "really?" I thought about what happened. When I pulled up, my ex was under the hood of our son's car and when he raised up his head from under the hood, he waved at us, and I waved back being cordial. My ex-husband didn't have any issues with Vincent, and yes, my ex would push my buttons from time to time, but this time we were cool, so why not speak back. I'm a polite person, so even if there's tension in the air, I will still be cordial.

Many times, we see things, we'll ignore them, and I did just that. I ignored Vincent's sarcastic mood swings and oh boy, was I in for a surprise!

Every time I was with Vincent, I loved it. Our endless conversations about God added to my love for him. He would tell me about the older men, telling me about how they had taken him under their wings and how they taught him so much as a young boy/teenager growing up. He would talk about how his mom (RIP) would iron all of his clothes for the week, and that was a pattern from his childhood. Grown, he stilled ironed a week's worth of clothes for work. There were so many great attributes and that's why I choose to stay with Vincent, even though he had lied to me about being married. Anytime he would hold me, oh wow the butterflies and I would just smile.

Mary Mason Foote

The Move

My son got into trouble at school. He and some little snot nose bullies were at it all the time fighting with one another. So, I decided it was best to move, so Starkville, MS it was. Vincent wasn't happy with my decision, but I went anyway. We were dating not married and I had to do what was best for my children. Although it wouldn't stop him from coming to see me. He would come to Starkville every night after he got off work.

The day of the move was so funny. I rented a U-Haul for the move. My brother, two male cousins, Earnest Mason and Ralfeal Brown my two children, and my son's best friend KJ, were there to help me pack up. My family is there for me every time I needed them. Vincent who I sometimes referred to as Mister, (when I see that his mood has changed) came to the house while we were packing (It felt like a scene from The Color Purple). Vincent came bouncing (he had a walk like George from the Jefferson swinging his arms) down the street towards my apartment with gorgeous puppy dog eyes. That was so funny to me, he showed me a side of him that had me like, "Really Vince!"

The look in his eyes was hurt, anger, and disappointment all at the same time. I would stop from time to time while packing just to pamper him and pat his ego. I had to let him know that I wasn't leaving him. I'm not thinking about meeting anyone else, and he was who I wanted in my life. He was concerned about me meeting someone else while in Starkville, but nope! He had captured my heart and made me feel secure, so I wanted to see where our relationship was going.

We finished packing (nope he didn't help, just looked) and Vincent was sitting on the steps like he had lost all hope. He sat there with a white t-shirt and blue jeans shorts. He had his hands resting on his cheeks with his elbows on his knees pouting and it was funny, but I held my laughter together until I pulled off! My brother and my cousins couldn't, they laughed, but Vincent didn't know what they were laughing about, but I did because they kept whispering in my ear "he's gonna cry when we leave." They were calling him "Red" from the movie Friday after Debo took his chain and he ran to his car, that's exactly how Vincent was looking sitting on that step.

Lord knows we had a really good laugh all the way to the new apartment and while we were unloading the U-Haul. My brother and my two male cousins are three men that will make you literally bust your guts laughing with them! My family is so funny and some very cool people to be around. We made it through the move laughing like we did when we were children. Now they loved Vincent like he was family, but the moving scene we couldn't help but be amused by it, it was funny, and it helped in the process (hahaha).

I got settled into my new apartment, and Vincent was there the next day. He had calmed down and got himself together, he was incredibly happy to see me and so was I. When a guy leaves a pair of shoes, you know what that means. Yep, marking his territory. He started off staying until the next morning to moving in. It's funny how we let things get out of hand, but my heart was involved. Still dating, hanging out as couples did, it was such a pleasure being with him night after night. My children didn't mind him being there. They just didn't like the slip of controls that he was trying to put in place. Other than that, they really honored what he would say to them and they valued/respected him as being their stepdad. There was never a time that my children disrespected him. Never!

Mary Mason Foote

The Green-Eyed Devil

We left the church and was heading back home to Starkville, MS. Vincent was driving behind us. We decided, the children and I, wanted to go out to eat, so I pulled over and told Vincent where we were going. He stared at me as if I had just told him that he couldn't join us. I was confused and asked, "Vincent, do you hear me? Let's go out to eat." He snapped out of his trance and said "okay." I get back into my car and pull off, then I heard tires screeching. It was Vincent driving crazy behind me. I pulled into the restaurant, and he pulled in behind us. He sat there not saying a word, so my children and my son's best friend went on inside. He finally got out of the car, came in and sat down with an attitude. I asked him "what was wrong", but he said "nothing." Well, that nothing was ugly!

Vincent wasn't too fond of me being with others or us out with other couples, and I couldn't understand that. Whenever we were out alone, we never had any altercations, he was always pleasant, and he treated me like a Queen. I remember one day when dining out with a friend and her guy, Vince was very nasty and he really showed his tail on me, in front of them. When we got home, I asked him what his problem was? His response would always be, "nothing." Hanging out with my friends or family would always end up in an argument when I got back home. As long as I was home and not with anyone, we were super cool, that was crazy!

It took me a while to figure out why he would get so

angry at times. Well, I was about to find out. That darn Bud Light, , I had no idea that they were inseparable. Beer wasn't his friend and it didn't look good with him. Vincent just couldn't handle it and it was a huge issue for us!

As I think about it, the liquor store has "wine and spirits" written on the outside of the building and it surely would manifest within my love, from nice to controlling! I hated that spirit so much, but I loved the man. We were in constant and unnecessary arguments that stemmed from the drinking. I need to encourage you. You, who are drinking or entertaining those spirits in the bottle, it will and can destroy you, your family and people around you. Please, if it's doing that to you, pray to God, to take that urge away. PLEASE STOP!

Holidays

There was a time I didn't care much for the holidays because it brought me so much pain instead of joy. Now with Vincent, the holidays brought me such joy. We spent our holidays together, shopping for others and barbecuing. Lawd that man could cue some meat. Our smiles seemed to complement one another. We both have hearts to show our appreciation to one another and for others. He always gave thought about what to buy, and whatever gift he bought it was always more expensive than mines. He was a man with great taste, and I wouldn't want it any other way, because I would do the same for him. Vincent made up for all of the horrible holidays in my past.

I didn't bash my last relationship; I wanted the real Vincent and not a mirage of "I'll be what she needs me to be." I wanted a fresh love, not one built on comparison and I got that. I never had to wake up to him leaving me on the holidays, him hiding his phone, no foolishness, he was always there, and I was spoiled by it. There were times when drinking his beer wasn't so bad, we would sit on the couch and watch TV. No arguments because we were both getting what we wanted, alone time together.

Mary Mason Foote

Getting to Know Him

Time passed by and we began to really peep one another out, his faults, my faults, his likes, and my likes. We were similar in many ways. I thought that I was clean, but oh no! I must say he kept a cleaner house than I did. Cleaning, washing, folding clothes and cooking (barbecuing) he was a notch better. Vincent would wash down baseboards around the floor, clean ceiling fans, wipe down beds, get way back in the corner cracks on the floor, he was so clean. Vincent had to put a shine on everything, and I loved it! We'll be at home in his own zone getting down cleaning, I would join in and we would laugh and talk like the best of friends.

Now when he started drinking a little too much, that's when I got a little silent. I knew that I would have to see that spirit that I had hated so much! I had been running from that intoxicated demon all of my life. That drunken spirit just makes my soul cringe. Looking at that spirit face to face was a challenge for me and I could literally feel and see the cold, clammy, sweat demon from hell. It was easy for me to identify the drinking Vincent, from Vincent whom I love and loved me back.

He couldn't understand why I would become withdrawn at times. I would cry and I didn't want him to touch me. I knew it was an ugly spirit manifesting itself, but he couldn't tell the difference. As time went on that spirit became a part of our lives and showed up quite often. The more comfortable he became at home with me being with him, the more conflicts arose. I became more withdrawn and he got angrier, it was ugly!

Once again, I started to die inside. I started hiding my feelings to keep the peace. It's a feeling from my past that didn't want to deal with it again. Vincent was everything I wanted in a husband, but I couldn't deal with the drinking, control, and jealousy. Drinking would make him act like a darn nut and that spirit would haunt me. It was as if that demon would say, "You thought you could get away from me" and there it was raising its ugly head, in the man that I LOVED PAST ETERNITY. I was reliving my past all over again. Eventually, I would have to deal with it head-on.

I started to get depressed, isolating myself. I would find myself rolled up in bed crying myself to sleep or in the shower, head up against the shower wall crying my eyes out! I was asking God to just take me if I have to live like this. The arguing and silent treatments from him were getting out of control. As long as there wasn't any drinking, we were perfect, but that wasn't enough. I couldn't allow him to be that version of himself because I saw the greater in him. I was miserable! When he moved in, that became his home too and I honored and respected that, but I couldn't deal with the drinking. I was never the type to get what she wanted and forget about the other person. I tried to help the situation by talking to a few of my spiritual mother's during his episodes. He didn't like that at all, that spirit that is.

See, spirits, and demons are real. Many take it as a joke. From the age of eight, I saw demonic spirits, but not fully knowing what was happening. What I do know is that it can't be ignored. It's best to operate in a five-fold ministry so that we can be taught, especially if you're experiencing activities in the spiritual realm. I began to understand that I was getting practice for future spiritual warfare. Sometimes I would ask Vincent, "were you sent on an assignment, did the devil send you to destroy me and stop me from walking in the call from God?" He would respond, "You talk like a foolish woman."

Our conflicts continued and they went north, south, east, and west whenever "Bud" showed up. Bud Light that is, problems bounced everywhere! No matter what, we argued. If I was with my family with or without him, we argued. One day I wanted to go to a concert, and I asked him about going with me and he didn't want to. He said he didn't mind me going, so I went, and Lord knows I didn't know it, but it was a setup. I was gone about two-hours and came back to a hell dungeon! He was so mad and gave me the silent treatment. This happened whenever I was with other people.

Whenever this happened, I would look in the garbage can and there it was! Yes, empty containers of bud and his friends in there, leaving my man acting a fool! I hated it because it brought chaos in our home and to the man that I loved. I decided I would talk to Vincent about his behavior and eventually told him about my past. That made everything so much better. He held me so close and loved me with a burning love within. That surely made me love that man of mine even more.

Mary Mason Foote

Going Deeper

After telling Vincent about my past things seemed to get better. We worked together trying to please one another. I went deeper into the word of God, and so did he. He has always been a church boy all of his life. He was an usher since he was a little boy, and he attended faithfully every Sunday. Very respectable even in his adult years, and here is the kicker, there was so much that I love about that man. I loved his walk, talk, dress, the way he opened doors just making sure that I was good, it was an emotional rollercoaster for me.

The more Vincent got into the word, the less he drank. He would read his bible for hours, so I thought it was going away. Nope! It was like bud and Vincent had made a deal. He became so clever with hiding it. Whenever we would go by the store, he was so good at hiding it from me and somehow, he'll pick Bud up and I didn't even notice it. My spirit man became stronger and more aware of the word of God, and it became harder to shake the way we were living.

When the spirit of the Lord really comes alive in your life, it's hard not to want to change. I was becoming so convicted in my spirit. Being lukewarm was bad and I knew that If I had died, hell would have been my destination. I was all over the place with my flesh, lust, and a heathen. I don't wish that tug of war with the flesh on anyone. Fighting sin and fighting to live in holiness is a struggle, but God!

God left neither one of us. I wasn't raised in the

church, so there were a lot of green moments for me. While we were dating, we would go to church together and I would be so observant and having a conversation within for many hours. I had so many whys and whats, that I would cry and be frowning at the same time through the service. God would show me visions and literally be talking to me about certain things all at the same time. After accepting my call into ministry, Jesus's school became so real in my life as I was becoming a disciple and a follower of the word of God. This happened despite my fornicating and shacking up. I was so ignorant, but God! I often looked at Vincent while he was on his ushering post and say, "how could you usher and you're not living a saved lifestyle, by shacking and getting drunk." I would question myself as well, "Mary what are you doing?" I wanted to please God, and that renewed spirit in me was screaming within, and it soon began to scream out into our home.

Lord, now that I think about it, the man didn't have any other choice but to drink dealing with me. I would constantly tell him about my spiritual convictions about us shacking and not being married; he didn't like that. His divorce hadn't been finalized yet and there was nothing that he could do about marriage, so he would get so angry with me. "I'M TIRED OF HEARING IT" was his favorite saying. He didn't say it kindly either, oh no! He would get so manly with it and I would shut up and let him calm down until the next day! Oh my, I was awful, but I couldn't help it. My soul was thirsty for Jesus. His teachings in the word made me crave the pure holiness of God. That yearning was brewing deep in my bones. Vincent would tell me to "hold on, just be patient" again, I love that man!

I Have to Get Out of This

The more I long to live Holy, the worse things became between us. An opportunity presented itself for me to have a one on one with someone who knew him very well. I was only inquiring about him because I wanted and needed to understand him better. That was a big mistake. It was a friendly conversation. Obviously, that person couldn't wait to tell him and put their own twist to it. I was so stupid to trust them, and now that I think more about it, they had good reasons for why they did what they did, even though I thought they were being genuine and would keep it confidential (that's what we agreed on). I just wanted to know what set him off as he would get at times and what was fueling his anger? They seemed extremely helpful, so it appeared that way because later they told him about our conversation. Oh man, he was terribly upset with me, even though they did most of the talking. I'm sure they made the conversation seemed so ugly, but all I wanted to know was, how could I try to make things better for us both (Vincent and l) again, A HUGE MISTAKE!

Later the same day we were supposed to go to our first day of marriage counseling, but after that blow-up, it was a no go (the devil stepped in). He hadn't proposed yet and there was no set date, but we both wanted to get more clarity about marriage and if we were right for one another. He and I both were hoping that God would do that for us, with this being our second marriage. After the huge fallout, he left the house, and it was over. He came back home earlier that night after he cooled off, and we tried talking, but I was still being convicted in my spirit. I was miserable with his drinking, jealousy and now he was upset with me for discussing him with someone else (I still want to slap them).

That same night I went to church, and when I got back, he was all in my face about me going. His trust issues were becoming more and more awful. I had no other choice but to say, "it's over." I couldn't take it anymore! I packed his bags and oh my God, did that hurt. Packing a man's clothes and putting him out is something that I would never suggest to a person. You may want to come to a mutual agreement with them before packing their clothes, let them do it and choose to leave peacefully. I often think about that incident, and it leaves me feeling so bad. When I would think about it, it's as if I'm uncovering a fresh wound. It was hurtful and embarrassing. It took me a while mentally to get over putting him out. I never meant to hurt him; I was just so tired of the turmoil between us.

Even after our fallout, we never stopped communicating. He moved, but we never stopped talking on the phone (two months split). I loved him just as much as he loved me. I apologized for what happened. So, we started being cordial with one another again, he came over one morning and that was it, our sparks were lit all over again. We held one another so close, and we began to talk about our future together. He kissed me on my forehead as he held me close, saying how sorry he was for what he had put me through. We decided to have lunch after that makeup session.

He was everything on my list to God. I guess that's why love kept pulling us back together. Love covers a multitude of faults, right?

Mary Mason Foote

Lunch

Vincent went back to his cousin's house, at least, that's what he told me. I called him after he left to see where we were going for lunch, and he said it's up to me. I chose The Grill in Columbus, MS for those good ole fried cheese sticks. I arrived first and as I sat waiting my phone rang. It was a friend of mine.

"Whatcha doing friend," I asked with a smirk in my voice.

"I'm in the mall and I see." She began, but I cut her off. God told me to interrupt and get off the phone with her and I did.

After I hung up, I called Vincent to see where he was, and he said he was still driving. After about five minutes later he walked in. He sat down beside me, and we ordered our food. After eating, we just sat there talking.

"Do you really love me," he asked.

"Yes," I replied.

He asked again "Do you really love me enough that one day you would marry me?"

"Yes, Vincent, when you're ready."

He looked down at his plate then looked back up at me. He pulled out a Zale's ring box! I took a deep breath and bucked my eyes. "Wow," I thought "Is this what my friend was wanting to tell me about seeing him in the mall", but God didn't want her to spoil the proposal for us. That's why He told me to get off the phone.

When Vincent opened up the box and showed me the ring, I was surprised all over again. My ring was beautiful and pretty expensive. He wanted nothing but the best and that's what he always gave me. I was so happy. We sat there smiling and kissing. The waitress came over in the midst of our happiness and I shared with her my proposal. She got excited and called the manager over. The manager shouted to the entire restaurant and everyone there was congratulating us. God once again made it a memorable moment for us both. They took our picture, blessed us with dessert and gave us well wishes.

I called and told my friend about the good news. She said, "I was trying to tell you, but you hung up." Anyway, she wanted to see the ring, so Vincent and I went to the restaurant where she was eating after we left the Grill. She was happy and loved the ring.

Things didn't change much even after all of the joy. I was still hopeful that we would be okay. I loved that man that much. I just couldn't make him relax, enjoy life, and live. Everything was fine as long as it was just the two of us, but my life consisted of so much more, family barbecues, hanging out with friends, or just hanging out for some me-time. All of those things resulted in an argument ninety-nine percent of the time.

I tried to reason with him. I would say, "You're good looking, and I don't get mad when you go." I didn't, even though he was gorgeous. He had a caramel complexion, big sexy eyes, juicy lips, good work ethics and a flattering wardrobe to live for. Many women looked and flirted with him, and I definitely can see why, but for as me being jealous wasn't an option, because he chose me. I accepted in my mind.

Though he was loyal, being with him started to have a physical effect on my mind, body, and soul. Being in LOVE makes you blind to the bad things. Some way we just keep covering the faults of those we love. Only a few people had an idea of the stress that I was dealing with. I began to develop eczema, hair started falling out and things were getting worse! I suffered in silence, not knowing if we were going to argue at any given time about absolutely nothing! No matter what, an argument was coming. I did find a way to end those arguments so that they wouldn't be drawn out for so long. I would say silly stuff to make him laugh, and it worked every time. Over time it became too much for me, trying to be happy and make him happy was entirely too much for me. When he wasn't upset, he was charming and knew how to love me in every way. That's why I endured the pain as long as I did.

We had a lot of funny moments in the midst of the madness, and some I must share. Vincent was so funny and clumsy. One day Vincent was meeting me and my children at movies. If I hadn't said it before, Vincent was always fashionably late, and this occasion was no different. He made it to the movie theater a few minutes after the movie started. My children Malik and Tyler sat a few rows in front of me (you know how teenagers can be), I spotted Vincent coming in and I waved so he could see me.

Now everything goes into slow motion. Walking up the stairs, so fresh and so clean as ever, all of a sudden, I hear a thump. He had missed a step and I could hear laughter coming from my children of course. He looked back at them, shuck his head, walked over to me, and sat down. After making sure he was okay he finally says, "yeah, I missed the step." I looked at him while in my mind, and wondered how? The steps were short and outright impossible to miss. Well after the movie was over and we were heading out the door, my child whispers in my ear and pointing "Mom, look."

I looked down and immediately the mystery of how my husband missed a step was solved. It was because of those long toe shoes he had on! I looked down and all I could think of was "Aladdin and his magic carpet." My husband and those Aladdin shoes couldn't make walking up the stairs possible! That was a fun night, even he had to laugh with us.

Happily, Ever after

A praying man is a sexy man. Vincent would pray until everyone in the house woke up. I used to get so mad at him about that. My children would be asleep, they had to go to school the next day and I had to go to work, but between three and four in the morning Vincent would go into prayer. None of us wanted to wake up to his loud prayers. I would ask him over and over again not to do that. He would just look at me and shake his head.

He had issues with respecting other people's space, especially if he was praying. God does come first, but this seemed to be done out of ignorance. God isn't the author of confusion, and there is a Golden Rule to respect. Matthew 7:12 whatever you would want men to do to you, you also do to them. It's a give and gets, but it got so bad with numerous things, that we eventually called it quits!

Months passed and I continued to figure out my life and what God wanted from me. Though Vincent wasn't there I never could completely let him go in my mind and heart. I tried, but he kept occupying my thoughts. We continued to see each other off and on. He told me that he had stopped drinking. This made me incredibly happy. He moved into his new apartment. Both of us were still very much in love despite the relationship issues. Time passed and he became unemployed. During that time, I tried to show him that I was there for him if he ever needed anything. He never asked me for a dime. He just wouldn't do it. What I did was when I saw a need, I didn't hesitate, and I just gave it to him.

Later, he got a call for a job in Houston, Texas. It was in October 2015. I was sad to see him go, but he was glad because he was used to making his own money. We would talk on the phone using FaceTime every day to catch up. He would tell me how good it felt to not be drinking and things were looking good for us. He still had my ring.

He asked me to put it back on three separate times. After the third time of asking me, I said yes. We were on the phone and he asked me to marry him. I said, "I would love to be your wife."

I realized I was trying to accept a will that I thought was what God wanted for me. I was wrong. So VERY WRONG! Jesus, I'm so glad for grace and mercy, those twins are amazing!

Vincent came home for a couple of days to Mississippi, but he didn't go home to his apartment, he came straight to mine and he didn't even tell me he was headed home, even though we talked on the phone until about 12 am. So early that morning, around 3:00 am, I hear a knock at my door, and it scared me. "Who is it," I asked. "Vincent," he replied. My eyes lit up like a lightbulb. Yeah, I was happy to see him! I opened the door, gave him a kiss and hugging him for dear life. I really loved that man! Vincent was not really good at executing a romantic event, but he would surprise me in his own little way. After going into the bathroom and picking his hair (he was about a month overdue for a haircut), he looked at me while I sat on the side of the bed with my legs folded. He goes into his black traveling bag and pulls out my wedding ring still in the box. He gets on his knee and asks, "You ready?"

"You have to ask me again," I said blushing. He looked at me, looked at the ring and asked again, "Will you marry me?"

"Yes!"

He slid the ring on my finger and just said wow! There it was, we are engaged again. We both were very happy!

He had to go back to work in Texas, so he let me do whatever I wanted and needed to do for as wedding planning. All the planning was totally up to me. He only had one suggestion; he would be picked his own groomsmen. We set the date for December 26, 2015. We had three months of no arguing and just loving one another. I would take trips to see him in Texas, check on his apartment in MS and whatever he needed me to do.

December 26th came, and I married the man that I love. The wedding was beautiful and more importantly, we were happy and finally husband and wife. I took his last name and it made him so very proud. A few days later, my husband had to go back to work in Texas. FaceTime was our best friend and absence made our hearts grow fonder.

Heartache hit hard though. I love my family. January 11, 2016, my mother's baby brother died without warning and fifteen days later, her baby sister, Aunt Mae, died. Those two deaths were unexpected! But God!

On the day of my aunt's funeral, February 6, I

witnessed a part of Vincent that I had never seen. At church during the funeral, he took on a spirit of arrogance. When I cried, he didn't console me, and he had never treated me so cold! After the funeral at the repast, my family was together, laughing and having a good time. My husband, on the other hand, just sat at the table looking mean and he says, "let's go." I looked at him and said "are you serious Vincent! My favorite aunt just passed and you're rushing me to leave my family." His response was, "I need to go read my Bible." I just looked at him while in my mind calling him crazy you know what. When I finally broke down and left, while driving he says, "you could've stayed. I would've come back to pick you up. I just wanted to read my Bible." Really, Vincent, I wanted to choke the crazy hell out of him!

Emotional Rollercoaster

Time passed and we decided that I would stay a week in TX, for Valentine's Day. I took the entire week off from work to be with my husband. We were still honeymooners. The drive to Texas was about ten hours, but it was worth it because I was going to spend time with my husband. When I got there, we booked a hotel room for a week. Vincent had a roommate, and he would never feel comfortable with me staying in an apartment with any guys, he didn't play that.

Everything was cool for the first day, but oh my! I woke up to Dr. Jekyll and Mr. Hyde. My husband's split personality! I would sit in the room crying my eyes out while he was at work and I thought to myself, "Mary just leave." I was about three days in, then my mom called out of the blue. I sucked up my tears, gathered myself, and answered the phone.

"Hey mom," I said trying to sound happy.

"You okay?" she asked being concerned.

"Yes, why you asked me that?" I said pulling the phone away from my mouth to let out a cry and gather myself again. The tears fell because the pain was so bad.

"I just wanted to hear your voice," she said, but I knew she was concerned and knowing that I wasn't okay. She wouldn't force us to tell her when something was wrong, even though my mom always had a strong intuition when it came to her children and others. I knew she felt something was wrong with me, and that's why she called. Even today when I think about that day, tears swell up in my eyes. I felt that I had made a huge mistake, but I had to deal with it.

Vincent came back to the room after work, and I fought back the tears and dealt with the pain. He sat there talking to me like nothing was wrong. I would look at him thinking what the heck is going on in his head. Though we were in a hotel, I tried to please my man, even going as far as cooking for him using a crockpot. After eating he would read his bible.

It's like the love meter had been turned off in his heart. Instead of loving me and making me happy, it's like he had been programmed to destroy me. I was so glad when that week was over. I was an emotional wreck and felt like I was literally in hell! It was an emotionless, loveless week and he literally didn't have a clue of how I felt. When I left, he kissed, hugged, and loved me like he wasn't going to ever see me again, what the heck! It was times like that, that kept me thrown off. He constantly called what seemed like every hour to make sure I was okay while heading back home to MS. It's kind of messed me up and made me question if I was over exaggerating and could it be in my mind. How can someone love and hate you at the same time? Very perplexing and just the beginning of my husband's bipolar ways.

Trying to Escape

I'm so accustomed to putting other people's feelings before mines. To me, everyone around me had to be happy by any means necessary and not being concern about my own well-being. I knew that I could handle whenever I would go through something because God would make it alright for my good and it would be okay. In my mind, I felt like I was the woman who was built to carry the hurt for everyone else, but that pain almost took me out!

It was the Fourth of July, and Vincent purposely picked a fight with me for whatever reason. We were supposed to go to his family house and of course, I didn't want to go by then, so he and his daughter went on. A client/friend called to see what I was doing. It took so much strength for me to hold back my tears to respond to her. I mustered enough strength, gulping a swallow in my throat that was now full of pain (that's when it's serious), I respond "nothing." She asked if I wanted to come over to eat and give her an insurance quote, I said that "I would love to come over." Saying to myself "it's better than sitting around crying anyway." During the drive to my friend's house, I was thinking happy thoughts and remembering something funny just to dry my tears away. I listened to some upbeat music, so by the time I got there, I would be my bubbly self. I was really broken deep down inside my soul! I hid the hurt, ate, and laughed with her family. Sitting there with her husband and their two daughters, I was so collected, no one knew the pain that I was feeling and that I wanted to cry, but God! I have always been good at hiding my pain and it had become normal to me. I was so used to it. I really enjoyed my friend and her family; the food was amazing! As we sat there talking, my friend's husband tells me that he works in the same line of work as my husband and that he knew him (construction workers). "Oh boy, don't let the tears fall" is what I was thinking as he begins to tell me how he knows my husband. Laughing it off through the pain. I made it! But as soon as I left her house and turned the corner, I let a river of tears flow. The dam had released a flood and my shirt was wet, while the ground was dry. When I finally made it home, Vincent was there. He was sitting in his chair as if nothing had happened. He never called to see where I was or to see if I was okay with nothing! Man did that hurt me!

I sat down, thinking as time passed by, then I had a thought. I was thinking maybe I could catch him slipping. I'll tell him I'm going to the store and hopefully, he would talk to the other woman on the phone. There had to be another woman, and I'll have my answers to why he was treating me so cold, it had to be because he was cheating.

I told him, "I'm going to the store" and he asked me to bring him back some ice cream. I said I "okay" hoping my plan would work.

I walked behind the chair he was sitting in, stooped down like I was tying my shoes, and slid my cell phone under his there. Yup! I'll catch him now! On my way to the store, my mind was everywhere, my heart was beating fast and I was anxious to get back to check my phone. The store didn't have his favorite ice cream, dang! I couldn't call to see what's his second choice, because I left my spying phone at home. I pondered and pondered what else I could get him. I grabbed his second favorite ice cream and went back home, after being gone for about thirty minutes, I was stalling to get an ear full.

I was tickled at myself when I walked in. Vincent was washing dishes. I was so nervous wondering about the phone and not the ice cream. I made up a conversation while trying to ease the phone out from under the chair. Babe this, babe that. Acting as if everything was cool. I tried my best to distract him and get him to sit back down. He walked towards the chair and saw the phone. Busted!

Oh boy, was he was mad. Heated and laughing at me in a taunting way while repeating, "You are a foolish woman! If you don't trust me, then we might as well not be together!" What did he say that for? I got back loud and hot with him.

"You're right, I don't trust you!"

"You're walking around here acting foolish, starting arguments, not paying attention to me, cold as hell and being nonchalant, you darn right I'm trying to see if you are cheating." I was equally mad and embarrassed. I had stooped to the lowest of the low.

He kept shaking his head and taunting me. I picked up the phone and pretended to delete the recording, right!

Nope, I went into the bathroom as I always did when he made me mad. I listened to the voice recorder. Listening to him talk to his dad on the phone and the TV was all I heard. I felt so bad and I never ever tried to snoop again. Not even on his phone. I knew God would show me, when or if he was cheating, I would know. God would definitely let me know; I've experienced it in a past relationship. Believe it or not, when he got in the bed, it was like everything was cool. Later in the middle of the night, here comes mister (wink). I was on an emotional roller-coaster that I would never wish on anyone else.

Moving

Vincent was later laid off from the job in Texas. I drove out there to help him move. As soon as that door closed, another job offer came the next day with the same company because he was a good worker. Of course, his bipolar ways kicked in while I was there! It started the second day, and like clockwork after sex, here comes the fiery darts. "Unleashing the Dragon" is what I would call it. If I was happy, you better believe we were going to argue.

That was it! I was done! I was crying, mad and upset because I couldn't please that foolish man! I wanted out and I wanted out right now! "When we get back to Mississippi, it's over" that's what I told him, and he knew from the tone in my voice that it was over! He could tell that I wasn't playing this time, I was fed up with his crazy ways! I was broken and I refused to deal with it anymore! Mentally, I was a wreck. My emotions were flying all over the place. As I helped him move and pack it was as if steam was coming from my ears like a chimney. I thought about the trips, the pain I had experienced every time I came to see him in Texas, and this episode right here brought more pain, and now I have to bring this one back with me too. I was leaving it all behind and leaving his crazy tail!

I thought about the church he attended out in Texas. Everyone there loved and respected him. Whenever I came, the people would embrace me and treat me better than he did. I had to front many times through my pain. They are an amazing group of people. The women of the church went as far as helping me plan a surprise birthday party for him, and he still was acting ugly that day.

There was another time when Vincent's daughter and I went to Texas to visit. It was a beautiful day, and we decided to ride the ferry and go to the beach. His daughter smiled and was ready to enjoy the ride and the drive to the beach. She and I were laughing, riding, and joking around, while he sat in the backseat mad for whatever reason. We got out of the car and Vincent just sat there with a frown! "Dude," I thought, "what is your problem now!" I kept saying "baby come on." He just sat there pouting and he said, "I'm okay." So, we left him in the hot car mad.

His daughter and I went to the top deck of the ferry. After a little while we looked up and there was Vincent looking for us. We laughed at his nonchalant stroll to find us. Finally, he spotted us, casually walking around the deck and he joined us. I convinced him to lighten up and have some fun. He finally relaxed a little and took selfies with us.

We went back to the car to head for the beach. His lips were poked out again. "Vincent, get out of the car and let's walk on the beach." He started acting stubborn again and wouldn't go, so we went on ahead and walked towards the ocean. I was laughing so hard because I took the keys with me, leaving him in the back seat hot and the windows up! That was hilarious!

When we got back to the car, he was gone. We waited in the car for him. He walked up and I asked,

"Where have you been baby?"

"Oh, I just walked on the beach."

Now that made me mad! We had been planning a walk on the beach for three years and finally, the time came, and this crazy man took that moment away from us. That really hurt me. All I ever wanted to do was love him and treat him like a king.

He made me feel so cheap with those silly unpredictable ways! There was a time I made that ten-hour drive to Texas even though I was exhausted, I pressed because we really wanted to see one another. Well, the morning came for me to leave and he was supposed to come to the room after work that morning to see me off, it was six in the morning and I still hadn't received a call from him. The wait seemed like forever! I finally called to see where he was, and he answered the phone. "I'm at McDonald's getting breakfast." He didn't ask if I wanted anything nor did he say that he was on the way.

While lying in that bed my heart dropped like a freight train that derailed. I let out a tear, shook my head, and asked myself, "How do I keep coming to see this crazy man?" I'm his wife, so why do I have to feel like the mistress? I got up and got dressed. I did an encouraging video for social media as I still do today. (I was good at putting my pain aside) and I went on my merry way.

Heart hurting, eyes full of tears that I wouldn't allow to fall. I had to get gas and food, refusing to allow my sorrow to affect another person's day. Afterward, honey when I got in the car, I started driving and cried a river. I also talked to God and I kept telling myself that "it's over." I imagined talking to Vincent about his behavior and how I wasn't going to put up with it anymore. In the midst of my thoughts, he called as if nothing was wrong. My intention was not to answer, but I needed him to know that I was strong. He and his narcissistic demon couldn't break me down! God had my back. If it wasn't for God, I literally would have lost my mind! Ladies never let a man take your will to live and live freely! You are fearfully and wonderfully made and God's blessing to man. A man shouldn't be our curse.

My pain was deep like a sketched scar into my soul! Why didn't he love me as I loved him? I would sit in church hurting. I would sit there looking upside his head in a disgusting way as he said amen to the preaching of God's word! I frowned inside my heart as he nodded like he was a perfect saint. I continued to tell myself I loved him though. In the midst of the madness, the kindhearted Vincent would show up. Those were the moments I would hold on to for dear life, moments like that. I just wanted to love him and be loved back. The funny thing is I ministered in the newspapers and on social media for years as I battled the mental abuse. Ladies, NO ABUSE IS OKAY.

Back to the move, and all that has been said, my husband's new job was in Crystal Rivers, Florida and I was left at home to sort out all of the things he accumulated while in Texas. In Crystal Rivers, it had only been about three weeks before he was calling for me to come to see him. He booked me a flight and off I went. At the airport and excited to see one another, he kissed me as if he was really glad to see me. He opened the truck door, carried my bags in and we had a really good time. Later we went out for dinner and again, we enjoyed each other's company, playing around and talking.

The next morning was fine, but that evening, of course, a day later like clockwork! There he GOES! Man, what was wrong with him? I kept asking him. Three days of misery! My flight was a round trip, but we made plans to drive to Mississippi for his family gathering, the next day, spend a few days at home and later back to Florida. Okay, Vincent gets off to work, I'm all packed and ready to go as he instructed me before he left for work that night. I have his items packed for the trip and mine, and there go his little horns. I said to him "baby, I'll drive you, just relax." Two hours in and I needed to make a pit stop. What did I do that for! As I was turning into the parking lot of the restaurant he wakes up and there's goes the attitude. We both went into the restaurant, but he came out before me. I see him standing by the driver's side door huffing and puffing.

"What's your problem?"

"Nothing, just give me the keys, I'm driving!"

"No, sleep a little longer, we have seven more hours to go, I'll drive."

He wasn't having it, so I gave him the keys! While he was driving his phone rang, he looked at the number, click to answer, but he didn't say anything. The man on the other end had an accent (he said hello), Vincent said hello back and pressed the end button. I didn't think much of it. When

I asked him why he did that, answering the phone but not talking. He got so mad at me!

"I hate you, I'm tired of you with your jealous ass," He said with so much rage and anger.

I didn't say another word for the next six or more hours. I put my earplugs in my ear, looking straight ahead and fought back my tears. All I could say to myself was, "Mary, it will be over soon. Get out of this marriage and leave this crazy-ass man alone!"

I couldn't control his stupidity. I was determined that when we left Mississippi after the gathering, I was not going back with him, but my clothes were still in Florida, and my flight was a round trip, so I had to go back with him. When we stopped at the store for gas, I went in as if I was by myself. I didn't say one word to him. He started talking to me like nothing happened! I knew he was crazy for real now. I uh huh him until he apologized. Even then I didn't have anything to say to him. We made it home, I showered and got ready for bed, Vincent was acting as if everything was okay. I was done for good after hearing him say he hated me. About two days later, we left Mississippi headed back for Florida. I gave him the silent treatment as he acted as if nothing was going on. Back at the hotel, we talked, I pretended like everything was cool, while in my mind holding on to my "I'm done promise." The next day he took me to the airport, said our "I love you" and I was happy to go back home.

Narcissist

While away at home, I continued wondering why? Why weren't we happy anymore? Why the disgust when it used to be baby, I love you. Why did the cuddling and soft kisses stop? Why was he so angry towards me? Why, why, why? Was he drinking again? As long as I acted dumb or needy, he was okay. I have been a beautician for over twenty-five-plus years, now he wanted me to stop and get a job at a bank. It was like he wanted me to be someone else. Maybe he didn't like me having my freedom of not punching someone's clock.

"Go get you a job, sitting at the shop waiting for heads," he said it in such a degrading way! He was really trying to break me down, but I wouldn't allow it. What was the real issue? I couldn't figure it out. How did he go from me being the love of his life to what the hell did I get myself into? He loved Jesus but acted like he hated his wife. He would say things like "I love you too much." I was spoiled by him materially, but I was paying the price mentally.

One day, God allowed me to hear the word "narcissist". I have never heard that word before or what it meant until I heard one of my clients say it. I asked her what it meant. Lord, she was describing my husband! After that, I learned how to deal with him, and it made everything better. I studied that spirit, and I began to master my emotions and not allow him to keep me in tears.

For what it was worth, I was determined to make my

marriage a happy one. I justified his bipolar ways. He did not ever call me names, talked about my weight, or criticized me in any way. It was like he just wanted to make my life miserable, control me and break my spirit.

You Never Know When It's Your Last Time

Vincent called me on Sunday and Monday, and everything was good. He tells me that he missed me so much. It has been about a month up until that phone call when his behavior begins to be much better. He was treating me so good that I would call my mother to tell her about it, I said "Vincent is treating me so good; something must be wrong. We laughed and my mother would say "praise God."

On Tuesday, March 20, 2018, my husband asked me to come to see him and Lord knows I didn't want to go because he was coming home the next weekend for Easter, and plus I didn't want to fuss we were finally in a good place, but I said okay. He called to wake me up at 3:00 am the next morning to see if I was on the road yet, but I purposely didn't answer because I was sleepy, and I had changed my mind about going. He called again hours later about 9:00 am and as I looked into his eyes while talking on FaceTime, he asked me what time I was leaving? I wanted to tell him that I wasn't coming, but I heard the spirit of the Lord say, "You never know when it may be your last time." Immediately I said, okay baby, I'm getting ready now. An hour later, I was on the road. The reason I was reluctant about going, was because I didn't know if he would try to tear down my spirit again, diminish my smile, take my joy, or whatever he could do. I just didn't get it! Anyway, off I went to Florida. Something had changed and hopefully, it won't be the same scenarios as the previous trips.

On my way to Florida, my husband called what seemed like every thirty-minutes. "Where you at now baby?" Was his question every time I answered the phone. He was very caring and concerned and wanted to make sure I got there safely. Something was going on with my tire, so I was sidetracked. I went to Walmart to check it out. I stayed there for about an hour in the service department. Vincent was patient with that. Things were different. "Baby, I have the room for you," he said, hurry up" I replied with, "Okay baby, I'm on my way. I'm driving." We would both laugh! I really loved that. That was all I ever wanted for us to be happy. I loved to see that man of mines smile and laugh. Whenever he would smile and laugh, my face would light up and I would have so much joy in my heart because of it.

I thought about things as I drove. I always told him to stop being so uptight and live. Live, laugh and love, baby live, laugh and love is what I would always say to him. "Girl gone" in a playful manner would be his response all the time. I was a good wife and he knew it. He preferred me not to be hanging out and going so much, he didn't like that at all. It's like those things would make him act so silly. So, when he would call at night, I had to be in the house on FaceTime, then everything would be okay between us. There were plenty of times when I would just be getting home when he called, I'll leave everything in the car, run up the stairs and hurry in the house, just to answer the phone or call him right back to avoid arguing. He had to make sure that I was home. Lord, I had a hectic time when I had to do that, just to please him and even though it was stressful for me, I did what I needed to do to please my husband. Jesus, he just had to make sure I was home and, in the house, or it was going to be trouble. That man of mines was something else and he knew it.

There was a family gathering on his grandmother's side of the family and he said a speech. Now this is so funny, as he gave reverence to God, and he said, "to my beautiful wife, I love so much", I wanted to fall out of my chair and hit the floor! I was so shocked and tickled. I wanted to say out loud to everyone, "he's lying, he's mean, and trying to fool you all like he's a great husband." I wasn't moved by that at all because I knew when we got in the car, he was going to bipolar land. Again, that's a behavioral trait of a narcissist and it's like fuel for their ego and they love attention. I still hadn't got accustomed to going with the crazy flow though.

I was brought out of my daydream by another call from Vincent, "I'm in the room, I'm about to take a nap and hurry up."

Mary Mason Foote

When It All Falls Down

After about twelve hours of driving. I wanted to surprise him by knocking on the door saying, "room service." But I forgot the room number, so I had to call him. Walking to the door, then I knocked, honey my baby met me in his birthday suit, looking like a newborn sexy grown man. Having the most beautiful skin, yes water did him good! We were really happy to see one another. He kissed me and back under the cover he goes. I was about to shower, then the familiar soft-spoken voice urged me not to shower, just get in the bed, and that's exactly what I did.

At that moment laying face to face with my husband felt different. He looked at me differently, then a kiss and he just rested his head on my shoulder in a way as he has never done before. I just held him and listened to the beat of his heart, though the tv was on playing in a low tone, all I could hear was the beat of my husband's heart. We laid there holding one another for as long as he needed it. Passionate kisses as he says, "I love you", just staring into my eyes down to my soul. Vincent looks into my eyes like he was literally searching for my soul. I smiled back, "I love you too, baby." His eyes, kisses and facial gestures said loud and clear unspoken words of apologies to me. Even though he didn't apologize for words, his body language and heart did. Resting his head on my chest, I continued with gentle strokes for on his head, rubbing my fingers through his hair and I said, "it will be okay baby." It's like he wanted to say something but didn't know how to say it, it was like his soul was making peace with mine. I now know, that was a spiritual moment and it was ordained by God.

Hours have passed after making love, my husband laid cuddled behind me, holding me all night and we fell asleep (I remember when I use to ask for forgiveness afterward, but God)! Around four in the morning or a little after that, he squeezes me again and says, "I love you" and I said, "I love you too Boo."

"So, you're not going to work today," I asked.

"No, I want to spend the day with you."

"I'm cool with that baby" I smile, and we go back to sleep.

His daughter called from school about an ROTC trip or something and a few minutes later, we made love again. We laid back down, but this time I laid behind my husband and held my man like we were literally in paradise. That night and morning were perfect! He turned over to look me in the eyes again to say, "I love you", I love you too boo. I rubbed my fingers through his curly hair something he loved for me to do. I kissed his forehead and he was really enjoying the attention. He rolled over so that our backs were touching, and he went back to sleep. As I laid there awake, I thought about how it felt so good to feel his skin next to mine. The sound of his soft snore was relaxing and peaceful to me, he was resting well. About thirty minutes had passed it was around eight in the morning and I couldn't sleep. So, I got out of the bed to grab my bible and just as I was heading towards the bathroom to read?

I looked back because I saw that my husband was holding his head and moving his feet under the cover.

"Baby, you okay?"

"I'm okay," he replied in a tone that told me he was hurting.

He tried to get out of bed, but he wavered trying to sit up and I rushed over to catch him because he was falling over and would have hit his head on the edge of the nightstand.

I had never seen him like this, he was always so strong. His speech became very slurred. He kept saying, "oh my head." I'm thinking maybe he has a headache because he was murmuring "pill,". I remembered him telling me that he always kept aspirins in his lunch bag. "Baby, do you need me to get you an aspirin?" I was scared to move because I didn't know if he would try to get up again. God led me to pray for my husband. I held him so close and embraced him. I held him up with all my strength and began to pray for him. For the first time ever at that very moment, I was the one he needed. I was his strength as his body rested on my shoulder weak as a lamb. He was helpless, but not hopeless. I was there.

I prayed and I heard him responding in agreement to what I was saying, it was like he was a little child finding comfort in his mother after scraping his knee. I wanted him to allow our marriage to have a chance to be amazing. I needed him to let me be the woman who carried his last name in honor of him. After we prayed, I laid my husband back down. He was still holding his head in so much pain. There was nothing I could do to stop the pain! I felt useless! I panicked and called my mom.

"Mom something is wrong with Vincent!"

"What is it?"

I finally calmed down enough to tell her what was happening, and she told me to call the front desk and have them to call the ambulance. I was scared to leave my husband's bedside. I didn't want him to fall because he was constantly trying to fight to get up. I needed to be with him every second. I ran to the other side of the bed and quickly called the front desk and they called the paramedics. I ran back to Vincent, still trying to get up. I hurried to put some clothes on my husband, I refused to let people see my love in his bare. Vincent was so cooperative with lifting his bottom so that I could slip his boxers and pants on. This is really hard to talk about, the man that is always so headstrong is now in a helpless state and not able to stand because the pain in his head, was so excruciating for him. Jesus!

Okay (sighing), I kept him alert by asking him questions, questions after questions and he answered me every time. Though his response and speech were slurred, he would answer me. I dressed him in a hurry, then I got myself dressed. The receptionist knocked at the door, she comes in and I asked her to watch him while I finished getting dressed. I continued questioning him.

"Baby, what's my name? "Mary" What's your

daughter's name? He answers, What's my children's name?" He answers, He answered correctly, and it was breaking my heart. "Baby you're going to be okay," he said "okay." I said, "I love you", (crying).

"Okay, I love you too," was his response.

I couldn't bear to see him like this. He had never been that sick. What hurt more than anything, was the fact that I couldn't stop the pain. The ambulance arrived to take him to the hospital. "Stand Up," the paramedics said, and I shouted out "he can't!" Baby don't fight, let the paramedics help you, my husband was in so much pain that it seems as if he didn't want to be touched. It was like "dead weight" as he laid on his stomach and now, I know exactly what people mean when they would say that when a person is unable to hold themselves up. The paramedics finally put my husband on the stretcher, still moaning and holding his head. Baby, I love you and I'm right behind you, "okay he says." I called my mom, his family, then my mom again and she helped me to focus better. I needed to gather our things out of the hotel room, just in case, it was a long night. I thought back to before we got married, how my husband loved me and treated me like I was a queen. Yes, he was jealous and controlling, but he respected and honored me as his lady.

I thought about how we would go out, catch a movie, how he opened doors and he was always at home no clubbing or in the streets, our many trips together and just enjoying each other. He would watch me as I slept and reassured me of his love. We had so many laughs, him calling me 'ole crazy girl." All those good times came flooding back to my mind. After a couple of hours in the waiting room, the doctor comes out to tell me about my husband, he didn't sound very hopeful, but "he's in the recovery room" he says. I asked, "when will he wake up or be able to go home?" The doctor just looked, he said I don't know, maybe a week, two weeks, I don't know. I finally go to his room, standing by his bedside holding his hand, smiling at him while he laid there. I let him know that everything would be okay. I thank God, that I wasn't alone. Two of Vincent's church members (his friend and his wife) were there with me. I didn't know what to ask the nurse that was caring for him, but Vincent's friend did. He asked a particular question in medical terms, even though I didn't understand the question, I definitely understood the reply and I wasn't ready for that news. I was being hopeful.

It was my turn to take care of him like he wanted to take care of me when I had my surgery. I knew that I would take care of My Vincent with every ounce of strength in me. All he had to do was relax and allow love to take care of him as he would do me. I was so hopeful as I patiently waited for my husband to open his eyes, a movement or something, but he never did.

The Last Breath

It was four-thirty in the morning, and I sat there staring at my gorgeous husband as he was resting in his hospital bed. I wanted him to open his eyes, give me a smile, squeeze my hand or something. Instead, I heard a cough and a gurgle in his throat like he was choking. I jumped up out of my chair and called out to the nurse. A male nurse came in so calmly. He grabbed a hose and started cleaning out my husband's throat. I watched him as his body vibrated in the bed, struggling as if he needs to clear his throat. His stomach moving up and down seemed to take so much effort. While the nurse was clearing his throat with the tube, his body all of a sudden it gave no response to what was happening, not even a flinched! Another nurse came in and checked the monitor, while the male nurse continued cleaning out Vincent's throat. The female nurse started pressing on my husband's stomach feeling all around like she was feeling for something. "What's that for," I asked. She ignored me and continued to press. The male nurse broke the silence and said, "well, we'll let the doctor explain it when he comes in." I looked and said to myself, "who does something and don't know why they're doing it?"

Six in the morning came and there was a shift change. I had to step out while the next person prepared to care for my husband. I didn't want to leave, I wanted forever, but they asked me to excuse the room for the shift change and I complied with their rules. I wanted to remember every second to share it with my husband after we got home. I wanted us to reminisce about how God had saved him. Since I couldn't stay, I decided to go ahead and go to his job and report to his supervisor that he was in the hospital. I knew he would've wanted me to make sure his job was secure. His supervisor gave me the information to call and report that he was in the hospital, so he could still get paid while being off work.

I was still tired from driving almost twelve hours from Mississippi, an hour, and a half to Tampa Florida (hospital) and then going back to his job site in Crystal Rivers, which was an hour and a half away. I was one tired lady. While driving to the site I called the hospital to check on my husband. The report was "he's doing the same, he has no reflexes in his body." This came from the new shift nurse. I told her I would be back in a few hours. I needed to get some sleep before I drove back, and her response was "okay take your time."

About three hours have passed, I showered, then I called his aunt to tell her what was going on. I told her I would give her an update once I got back to the hospital. After we hung up my phone rang again.

"Mrs. Foote," the nurse on the other end of the phone line.

"Yes ma'am," I responded.

"How are you doing?"

"I'm well, and you?"

"Oh, I'm doing great, thanks for asking. I'm calling

because the doctor is in, and he wants to speak to you. How long will it take for you to come back in? I know you told me that you were going to nap for a few hours, so I'm just checking."

"I'm on my way," I replied (still no sleep)

"Okay but take your time. There's no need to rush."

I didn't like how she said that. Take your time. I called his aunt back, told her about the phone call and I headed back to the hospital. An hour later, the nurse called back. I told her that I'd be there in about forty minutes and once again she tells me to take my time. I was like, "why does she keep rushing me then?!" I stopped at Wal-Mart to get some gas and some comfortable pants because that hospital was cold! While checking out at Wal-Mart, the nurse called again.

"Mrs. Foote, where are you? You told me you would be here in about forty minutes and the doctor is waiting to see you."

I let her know I was right around the corner and that it would be about 5 minutes.

"Okay but take your time and we will be waiting on you."

As soon as I turned the corner to walk into my husband's room, the doctor was on my heel. That was freaky! He introduced himself and asked me if anyone had told me exactly what was going on. I said to him "no sir, they haven't." He shows me the x-rays, pointing at my husband's brain. He pointed out the shifting (which was very clear to see). He explained everything to me in such a calm voice making me feel so hopeful, then turned around and said, "he's braindead, there is no activity and I'm sorry for your loss."

"What, wait, wait, wait," I yelled, "you mean to tell me that my husband laying here is brain dead and he's gone!"

"Yes," he replied, WHAT! The doctor then turns to console me with a hug me, but I ran into the arms of one of the pastors of the church where my husband was attending. I cried, but quickly began to tell about the goodness of Jesus and how amazing He is! Looking at my husband laying in the bed, I knew he was dead, his eyes were dry and jelly looking half opened with no movement. I begin talking about his life and how much he loved Jesus!

As he laid there, I'm smiling looking at my love, my arms folded and nodding my head. I see him praising God, in a vision with hallelujah praise!

Jesus. Seeing that vision of him clapping his hand, gave me comfort. I looked up and the nurse was standing by his bedside crying and just looking at me. She says, "you're so strong I just want to hug you." I walked to the other side and hugged her. The nurse was crying harder than me as I comforted her. My love for God is so deep, that's where my focus and strength rely in and upon. I truly believe, those who love Jesus and live according to God's words, when they die, they will be with the Lord away from this world. It's giving me great joy, as I think about Jesus! Oh wow, Vincent's daughter and his grandmother, man! I felt numbness, puzzled as if the earth was still and time has been put on pause. The doctor, where's the nurse and the pastor? all were gone, just a beep, beep, the beep is all I could hear. No thoughts, no movement just standing there still looking at my husband. While standing by my husband's bedside, in walks two ladies and my trance was immediately broken as they asked me to walk with them. I did and we walked down two long hallways then finally into a room. We sit down, they tell me who they were and asked me if my husband was an organ donor? I looked, said to myself, "I know they didn't take me away from my husband's bedside to talk to me about his organs!" Yeah, they were nice, but I didn't appreciate it, and this wasn't the time. I was upset! I listened for a few minutes and I interrupted, "can we finish talking in my husband's room? I want to go back to him." They looked at one another, then back at me, "yes oh yes" as they replied as if no one has ever interrupted them as I did. All I could hear was "blah blah blah's as their lips were moving, but not a word of English (laughing now as I think about it) I'm paying them no attention, just thinking about my husband, laying in that bed, "is he really gone?"

    Walking back, I felt more like sprinting, the blah blah blahs in the wind as they continued talking, but my mind was in the other room. You should've seen them trying to keep up. I thought about what they were saying as we were walking. I stood by my husband's bedside, opening up his eyes and just staring at him. His tongue was visibly swollen, his eyes were dry and gummy looking. I knew he was no longer here with us. I cried in silence and talked to God.

At four-thirty in the morning, to me, I believed that's when my husband died. The nurses wouldn't tell me what was going on with him, but that's what I believe. Vincent's body was there, but he was gone. I squeezed his hands, closed my eyes waiting for a hand gesture or something, still nothing! I finally responded to Life Link about donating his organs. The ventilation machine was still attached to him after he came out of surgery. As they explained and talked, I never took my eyes off my husband's eyes, hoping he would move, flinch, and just give me some sign of life, but he never did.

"Don't touch his eyes, I love his eyes, I told them. Don't touch his skin, oh how I love his skin. Don't touch his face, lips, teeth… just don't butcher my husband."

"Please don't destroy my husband, and don't send him back to me, like a science project." I believed I scared them because their smiles were gone when I said that in a serious tone. "Yes, he's gone, but he's still my husband," is what I told them. They assured me that they would treat him as if he was their loved one, and as if he was still alive.

Phone Calls and Funeral Plans

Getting my husband back home to MS was a small challenge, but God! The funeral home in Florida wasn't notified that my husband's body was ready for pick up and that was five days after his death (bummer). By Wednesday Florida had picked up the body and Thursday Mississippi was doing what they do best. Both funeral homes were amazing as they worked together ensuring that all was well. My husband's body arrived giving the funeral home in Mississippi just enough time to prepare for the viewing Friday afternoon at 12:00 pm.

I tell you, the way they made sure that my husband looked as if he was sleeping is an understatement! I told you all earlier, my husband had to be fashionably late and he made sure he did it one last time before his physical body was to be laid to rest. Everything I hoped for and imagine was delivered by God, through them.

My daughters were there with me, being by my side making sure he was put away in style, just like he was when he was living. I thank God, for them (you need the young and mature on your team, their vision is PHENOMENAL)! One suggestion from us for as the theme, that was it and the funeral home took it from there.

Now, the very day of viewing, I had no idea of what to expect concerning my husband's casket. I knew what to expect with his attire because I picked it out myself. Let me tell you about his attire. Vincent had been holding on to this royal blue suede suit jacket for about two years and I use to ask him all the time "baby why haven't you worn that jacket yet?" His response would be every time I ask him "I'm waiting on a special occasion", well, when I walked in our bedroom closet God reminded me about that jacket again, "the time is here and the special occasion was now." That's what I heard from the Lord. Even in the casket, my love had to be sharp! People would often say to my husband "boy you know you look casket sharp" if casket sharp as a person, then he was it! My husband's favorite team was the Dallas Cowboys, and he would always talk about how he wanted to go to one of their games, but never got a chance to go or shall I say, "make plans to go."

Back to the day of my husband's viewing. I had no idea, yet I had requested, but still, no idea what I was going to see when I finally got a chance to see my husband for the first time since March 23, 2018. The funeral director (I have always liked her spirit but now, I LOVE her spirit and we have become God's ordain sisters and friends) kept telling me to relax and that I would be very pleased, "trust me, you won't be disappointed" she said that all the way to the viewing area door. Okay, nervous and scared, because if I didn't like what I saw, it would've been too late to change it and I would have failed my husband. In my mind, I couldn't stop his pain, even though in the past I was able to do all that he had ever asked of me, but I couldn't stop the pain he was enduring. Jesus, that moment in the hotel room as my husband held his head moaning "oh my head" still plays in my mind, even today.

Okay, if I didn't like it, I probably would have lost it and sat on the floor pouting like a child (that's how I express my anger). Here goes, she says "stand here and don't move." She walks out of one door and minutes later she says "okay" at another door and oh my God, my eyes bucked, and I couldn't say a word! The team of people who worked so hard to deliver what I asked of them, made me cry. There lies My handsome husband in his royal blue suede jacket inside that beautiful blue Dallas Cowboys theme casket. A picture of the Dallas Cowboys Stadium on both ends of the casket, and on top of it was a picture of my husband with his hands in pockets posing like he is saying "I look darn good" and he did look good in that suit. A headshot of that same picture, as a construction worker and as mister GQ wearing one of his many hats (he loved stylish hats) were displayed on the outside of the casket, it was breathtaking!

Looking as if he was asleep. My words to my husband as I looked down at him in the casket was "baby, now you finally get to go to the game." It was absolutely beautiful!

Flowers that were sent from Florida and Texas, and from many other people who knew my husband and considered him to be their friend was beautiful surrounding him. The homegoing celebration was the heart of Vincent, with God's divine perfect plan. My mother and two sisters made sure I didn't have anything to worry about when it came to his obituary write up, those ladies are sharp and very smart. Lord knows I thank God, for my support team. Oh my, when the funeral director gave me the obituaries (identical to the Cowboys theme) there was another head-shaking moment of mines. I cried and I hugged her with so much love, I thank them all for being so caring, considerate, and very professional in handling his remains and the pictured perfect viewing of my husband for the last time. I'm sure my husband probably was over them all, "do this, do it this way, no man hold it steady, now now now, I I I got to be right" (whenever my husband got excited, he stuttered). Laughing and imagining him being just like that, played in my mind. Yeah, he was funny when he wanted to be. I'm so thankful for My family, my friends, his friends, my clients, his church family, and mines.... for making sure all was well. Lord, I thank God, for all of those amazing earth angels.

The day of the funeral was tough, but I was strong through it all. Standing outside the school's gymnasium where the funeral was being held, was really tough, but God! My daughter was there right by my side, holding my hands as we pressed through. The funeral director again amazingly, took care of everything from the beginning to the end. Absolutely amazing and that helped my aching heart full of tears due to the hurt I felt within towards many because of how some hurt and disappointed me, due to lies and disrespect. Dealing with death and feeling like you're hated by many, takes a person of faith to handle that type of pressure, with grace to keep it moving and I did, it was ALL GOD'S GRACE and MERCY.

The funeral director took me by the hand and I never let go of my daughter's hand. Standing in front of the line where I was supposed to stand as his wife, who honored, respected, and was devoted to her husband. I stood proud, because of God's grace and mercy through it all. The good times and the bad times, I was able to stand. Vincent's best man that was in our wedding looked back, waved, and stepped out of the pallbearer's line up and gave me a hug. That only hug, even after I drove up at the funeral, gave me life. Hmm, I was like pinky from Friday, before that hug "this wasn't going to break me down, I was Mary, and I had to stay strong", but that hug really blessed my soul. God is my refuge!"

The funeral director was so professional, compassionate, organized and about business. She escorted the grandparents in and after they were seated, she began the funeral processionals. I still get tears in my eyes when I think about how she intervened several times on my behalf as the wife for my husband's home going. I wasn't intending to speak at the funeral, but God when He says speak, you speak. I was led to addressed whoever in a beautiful way. I acknowledged and I let everyone know that was there, Me being married to Vincent was tough and that he and God taught me how to be strong and handle people with grace. I needed to let whoever know that day before we left, that God, has spoken and my husband's life here on earth was finished because it was God's decision and not mines. Only God has the right to give life and take it away.

At the burial site, tension and disrespect once again, white artificial rose, after artificial rose passed all around me (still smiling), but there was one of Vincent's relatives who thought enough to give me a rose for his casket, and for that I'm thankful. God will use just one, just one to soothe the pain and he did just that!

I'm reminded of this passage of scriptures

Psalm 91:7-16
A thousand may fall at your side,
And ten thousand at your right hand.
But it shall not come near you.

Only with your eyes shall you look,
And see the reward of the wicked.

Because you have made the Lord, who is my refuge,
Even the Highest, your dwelling place,

No evil shall befall you,
Nor shall any plague come near your dwelling.

For He shall give His angels charge over you,
To keep you in all your ways.

God's angels kept and inspired me to show acts of compassion so that I could, and I would keep the ways of the Lord, and that's to love everybody, regardless of how they treated me...

I love my husband and I miss him so much!

The hurt, the pain, the sadness, and the countless collections of tears that I endured in my marriage, was the MUDSLIDE, that I survived, that was meant to take me out mentally, physically, and spiritually.

My God is a keeper, Jesus interceded for me and I'm forever grateful for the comfort of the Father, the Son, and the Holy Ghost. Without the three, I would have not stopped sliding down the pit of despair. "I ENDURED it, I MADE it and I SURVIVED the Mudslide!

Mary Mason Foote

Plague Thoughts

I'll never know why after we were married, why things turn for the worst. Wondering if he had ever stopped loving me, was I getting on his nerves, did he feel like I wasn't good enough, was I pretty enough, smart enough, did I dress to his liking (he was sharp), did I speak correct grammar or as an embarrassment to him, was I a horrible cook, etc. I can go on and on with the negative whys (tears), but I'll never know. My answers are in the grave unanswered and only God can comfort my mind. I would often ask Vincent at times, "baby what's the problem, do you still love me?" He would look at me, literally in my eyes (on the phone or in-person) and say, "I love you too much." Even now and then, I take deep breaths with tears in my eyes, saying "he loved me, he just doesn't know how." I need to encourage you if you ever find yourself in a similar situation as I, I want you to know that God is definitely there in the midst of your hurt and pain, He will give you comfort and the grace to stay or walk away and live your life with your (reasons) decisions.

I know that love isn't supposed to hurt 1 Corinthians 13:4-7 and love is real, yet people are who they are, and you can't change them. Many times, there is a deeper truth that lies within a person, their actions and why they are the way they are. Some will tell you and some will just let you wallow in their pain destroying you without a clue of what they are doing to you and your heart. You raise your moment with Almighty God, you hide in the cleansing blood of Jesus and let Holy Spirit led you into what is

God's perfect will for your life. Be encouraged and know that Jesus is with you always and He's the reason (access) God hears your prayers and why you're never alone, for the Comforter is with you always John 14:26. Your Bible is your best weapon, use it...

About the Author

Mary Mason Foote was born on January 6, 1973, in Macon, MS. She's the second oldest of four siblings and I have two children a son and a daughter. A 1991 graduate of Noxubee County High School in Macon, MS and also an Alumni of Mary Holmes College in West Point, MS where she receives her degree in cosmetology in 1993. She became a salon owner "beauty of color" in Macon, MS immediately after receiving her degree and became a licensed hairstylist in the state of MS. Divorce, remarried and now a widow she's currently living in New, Albany. She was called by God, into the ministry in 2007 and licensed as an evangelist on June 3, 2012. She's a humorous, loving and very outgoing person that loves people. Seeing people happy, smiling, and living a life pleasing to God, that brings her absolute joy!

Mary Mason Foote

Epilogue

I've always been the one to carry the burdens of others, even as a child.

Nevertheless, something in me just loved. I now know that it was the love that came from nobody but God. He has always been there for me. Forever on God's mind. Jesus said, take my yoke upon you and learn from me, for I am gentle and humble in heart, and you will find rest for your souls. For my yoke is easy and my burden is light." (Matthew 11:29-30) This is something that I've learned as I grew as a follower of Christ.

My teenage years weren't that bad, although I felt like an outcast. That added to my pain and isolation, but I really didn't care. I hadn't made many friends in Chicago either, so when I moved to Mississippi at fifteen it didn't change anything. I didn't fit the click squad. My childhood was fun though. We never wanted for anything. My mom would say otherwise, but the four of us kids never knew the difference. That is until one Christmas when we didn't have a Christmas.

My brother, I think it was a Christmas when he was eleven years old, was determined to make a Christmas for me and my two sisters. He worked for my mom's cool friend and neighbors who worked the flea market every Saturday morning. Sure, enough Christmas came, and my brother used the money that he has saved from working to buy gifts for me and my two sisters. I'll never forget that day. My brother came into the house with a black garbage bag bearing gifts for us. We were so happy. My brother was AN AMAZING BIG BROTHER. He protected us, girls, at all costs. He has since gone on to be with the Lord. 9/19/2019 I have no doubt of where his soul laid to rest. Santa stopped coming for me at the age of eleven I believe, and, in all honesty, it didn't bother me anyway. I thank God, for my parents as they are the best!

I remember being around nine or ten, and our family was at the beach. My mom told us not to go too far out in the water. Somehow, I lost my grip in the sand and was taken away by the waves in the water. I was drowning, sinking to the bottom of the ocean. I remember clear as day something (I thought was a mermaid) pushed me back up to safety. I now know that it was one of God's angel that saved me.

After I got out of the water, I was too afraid to tell my mom what had happened, because I was afraid that she would whoop me. Even now, I never go past my knees in the ocean. I often think about that incident, and it gives me joy that God thought enough about me to save me from drowning. The reason I mention this is because I have always been protected by angels.

I've learned that no matter what is or has happened, Father Almighty God is still in control. He turns our tears and trials into testimonies. 3T's are what I call it! So many things have tried to kill, steal, and destroy me physically, mentally, and spiritually, but God. He always protects, comforts, and holds me as His very own daughter.

I have gifts and had visions at a young age. Repeatedly

they have come to pass in seconds of happening. I remember at eight years old, sitting outside our apartment building in Chicago. I heard a voice tell me, "Go in the house, kidnappers are out." I obeyed, and I went inside. A few minutes later my mom was telling us about a child that got kidnapped in the neighborhood. I thought to myself wow, that's why I had to go into the house, and still today I'm uncomfortable with seeing the red, green, and black Africa ribbon because of those colors associated with that time to me.

Another time, sitting outside on the doorsteps of our apartment building at the age of ten I heard, "Go in the house." It was the same soft voice. Sure, enough as soon as I went in and closed the door. Some guys were running in the building with bats, rakes, and a machete chasing a guy who lived upstairs in the same building. If I hadn't moved off the doorsteps, I probably would've been trampled. I can still hear my mom's voice screaming "Where are my babies?"

So, you see, God protects us, and He loves us. He gives us a warning, but do we listen to Him? Listen to that soft voice, that whispers in our ears.

Oh! Chicago was getting pretty rough especially for teenagers. My parents had two in high school and one on their way. One with her loud/smart mouth and feisty attitude. She never started a fight, but she wasn't backing down either, even if you looked like you wanted to fight her. A person would have to deal with her if they wanted to fight me, very protective, oh she was ready. My sister,

Tonya! WAS LIKE THE TASMANIAN DEVIL!

That being said, my parents knew what was coming when it came to my sister. So, they decided to move from Chicago to Mississippi to protect us from gang bangers. Being overly concerned about us fighting every day in high school. My younger middle sister Nikki was on the way to join us, and the mouth that my sister has, my brother and I possibly would have to fight every other day. So, we moved to Mississippi concerning fights. I had the toughest fight of my life, Lord knows I didn't want to, but I refuse to let a person kick me in my back and not defend myself. Let's get it! In the eighth-grade walking home from Benjamin Banneker Elementary School, minding my own business, the school bully said: "There she is!" He was referring to my sister with the mouth, but he thought I was her. He kicked me so hard in my back, next thing I know I was slinging him all across the sidewalk. I whooped him so bad that he begged me to stop. I beat his butt all the way to our apartment building!

I couldn't stop because I was mad, I was so mad that I didn't feel when he bit me on my breast until it started hurting and I saw the bite mark later on. After I finished with him, my friend kicked his butt too. While she was whopping him, and I ran into the house to get a butter knife. My Aunt Mae, rest in peace, asked me "what was going on" as she took the knife out of my hand. By the time we made it back outside my mom was pulling my friend off that same boy. He never messed with any of us again! I guess being a bully and getting whooped by two females in one day, was enough for him. Yeah, he may have bitten me on my breast while I had him in a headlock, but I had to beat him. He was hollering and I'm still laughing about it over thirty plus years later. Moving to Mississippi was the best thing my parents could have ever done for the four of us.

Adjusting to the country life wasn't so bad. In my mind, I thought that the kids at school would be country. Boy was I wrong. They were just as fly, maybe dressed even better than us in Chicago. I kept to myself at school, was observant, and went with the flow. My mother would always have a home-cooked meal ready for us every day when we got off the school bus, except for the weekends Friday through Sunday, we were eating bologna ha, ha, ha. I ate bologna what seemed like every day and forever! We ate bologna, crackers, and stage plank cookies so much, that I don't eat bologna right to this day.

Sometimes we would eat at the cafe down the road from our house and those were the best burgers! We would play pool while we waited, then we'll sit down and eat, full and smiling! Wow, moments like those are the best memories. As we matured and have our own families, those bad moments turn into happy moments. Anything that happens in our life is a learning experience and should make us greater. I'm forever thankful for God's grace and protection. Jesus is the reason I'm alive today and pressing through the good, bad, and ugly NO MATTER WHAT!

Grace beyond the grave

One more thing as I completely close this chapter of my life. Vincent was a man of great faith who loved Jesus, with everything in him. In no way will I take that from him, that was his life's devotion to please the Father and show others the way.

In his ignorance (not knowing any better) and later what I feel was his resentment towards me. In his resentment of having to readjust and change in order to move forward in our lives, the enemy took advantage of that secret hidden feeling in his heart. I knew he loved me, without a shadow of a doubt! However, there are things deeper than the eye can see and the mind can comprehend. Having a heart for someone that you love unconditionally, gives one strength to look past it all...